SCIENCE **DISCOVERY** TIMELINES

KEY DISCOVERIES IN
LiFE
SCiENCE

CHRISTINE ZUCHORA-WALSKE

LERNER PUBLICATIONS ◆ MINNEAPOLIS

FOR MY DAUGHTER MARIA, INTREPID BUG-CATCHER, PLANT-COLLECTOR, TREE-CLIMBER, PUDDLE-JUMPER, POTION-MAKER, AND QUESTION-ASKER

cover image

A white blood cell (in green) attacks tuberculosis bacteria. In the 1670s, Antony van Leeuwenhoek was one of the first scientists to see blood cells under a microscope, though he didn't have the technology to differentiate between red and white blood cells.

Content consultant: Kevin Finerghty, Adjunct Professor of Geology, State University of New York at Oswego

Lerner Publications Company
A division of Lerner Publishing Group, Inc.
241 First Avenue North
Minneapolis, MN 55401 USA

For reading levels and more information, look up this title at www.lernerbooks.com.

Main body text set in Diverda Serif Com Light 11/14. Typeface provided by Linotype AG.

Library of Congress Cataloging-in-Publication Data

Zuchora-Walske, Christine, author.
     Key discoveries in life science / by Christine Zuchora-Walske.
          pages   cm. — (Science discovery timelines)
     Summary: "Explore this fascinating timeline history of life science! What are cells, heredity, evolution, ecosystems, and photosynthesis? Who first studied these concepts? And who later built on and expanded the work of those early thinkers?"—Provided by publisher.
     Includes bibliographical references and index.
     ISBN 978-1-4677-5786-7 (lib. bdg. : alk. paper)
     ISBN 978-1-4677-6159-8 (pbk.)
     ISBN 978-1-4677-6250-2 (EB pdf)
     1. Life sciences—History—Juvenile literature. 2. Discoveries in science—History—Juvenile literature. I. Title.
QH309.2.Z83 2015
570.2—dc23   2014022616

Manufactured in the United States of America
1 –BP – 12/31/14

CONTENTS

INTRODUCTION

Life science, or biology, is the study of living things. Biology has a complex, captivating history. That's because it tells the story of humans' efforts to understand themselves and the organisms around them.

The earliest studies of living things were informal observations by ordinary folks working hard to survive. People learned about their local organisms to stay alive. What they didn't understand, they chalked up to gods and goddesses or other supernatural influences.

The first formal scholars of biology were probably ancient healers and embalmers from China, India, and the Middle East. However, most historians say the Greek thinker Aristotle changed biology from a practical pursuit into a serious field of study. Aristotle's writings include extensive discussions of the processes and stages of animal life. His student Theophrastus wrote similar works on plant life.

Aristotle and other biologists before about 500 CE were mostly observers. They noted the physical traits and behaviors of organisms. Arab scholars later studied their ideas, passing them on to thinkers through the Middle Ages (about 500 to 1500). Many of these observations were at least partly correct. But the explanations for these observations were often partly or wholly wrong.

In the 1700s and the 1800s, scientists began rejecting the idea that divine intervention plays a role in biology. They realized that the processes happening inside living things offered a more consistent and logical way to explain life. Scientists also began to explore the world, taking scientific expeditions that widened their view of nature.

Modern scientists have uncovered several key concepts that explain much of life on Earth. Cells are the basic units of all living things. New organisms arise from old ones, which pass their physical traits along through heredity. Evolution through natural selection determines which traits survive and pass on to future generations. And as time continues, Earth and its inhabitants will continue to influence one another. These discoveries came by way of many scientists over thousands of years, each scientist influenced by those who came before.

The first skilled pharmacists were Arabs living in Baghdad, Iraq, in the mid-700s. They made their own medicines to treat illnesses and other medical conditions.

A Line That Shows a Story

A timeline is a picture of history. It shows a series of events and their dates along a vertical or horizontal line. Timeline entries share a theme or a time period. Entries are always listed chronologically—in the order that they happened.

A timeline tells a story about a topic by placing key moments related to that topic in a logical sequence. It also helps people understand the cause-and-effect relationships between events. A timeline can span thousands of years or just a few minutes. Pictures often illustrate the entries in a timeline. Events that occurred before a certain point in history (in Christian tradition, the birth of Jesus Christ) typically include the abbreviation *BCE,* which means "Before the Common Era."

A series of timelines is one good way to tell the complex story of biology. Each timeline in this book shows how scientists are linked in their efforts to understand life on Earth. Each chapter in this book begins with a timeline, which shows a piece of life science history visually. Each timeline is followed by a story, which explains the history in words. Readers can check out the timelines first and then read the stories, or they can approach the stories in each chapter before examining the visual depiction of each story.

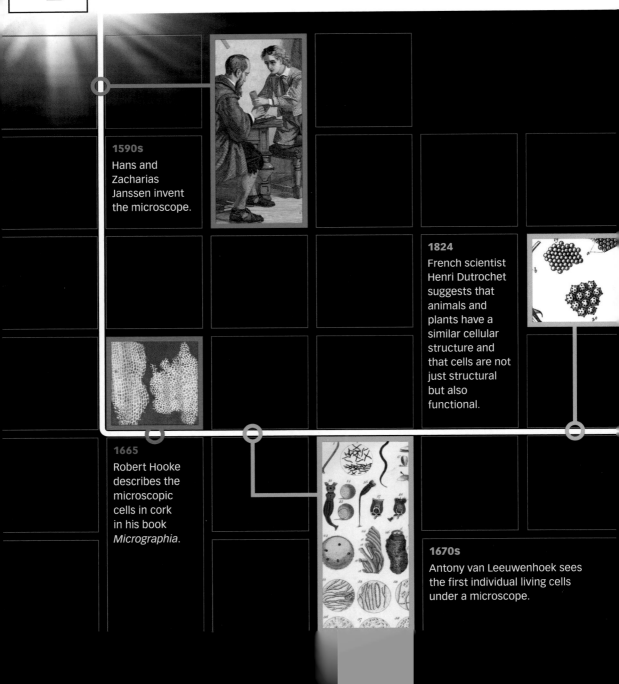

1590s
Hans and Zacharias Janssen invent the microscope.

1824
French scientist Henri Dutrochet suggests that animals and plants have a similar cellular structure and that cells are not just structural but also functional.

1665
Robert Hooke describes the microscopic cells in cork in his book *Micrographia*.

1670s
Antony van Leeuwenhoek sees the first individual living cells under a microscope.

CELLS

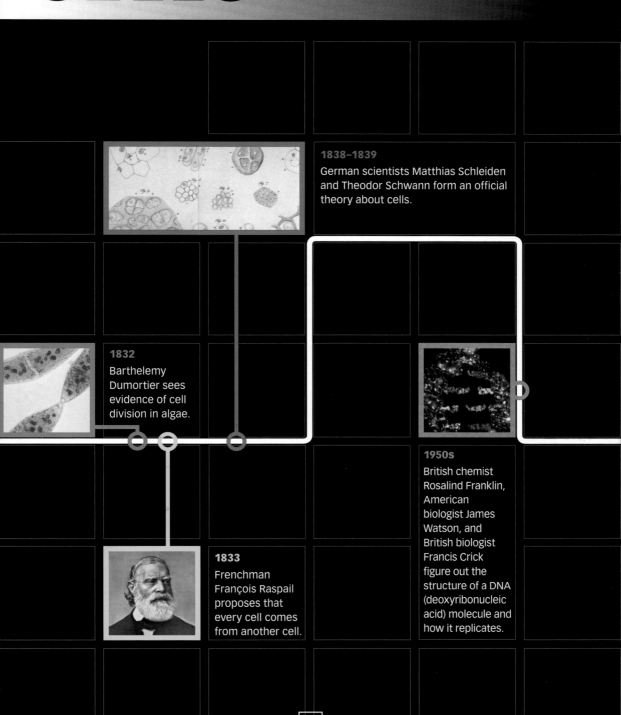

1838–1839
German scientists Matthias Schleiden and Theodor Schwann form an official theory about cells.

1832
Barthelemy Dumortier sees evidence of cell division in algae.

1833
Frenchman François Raspail proposes that every cell comes from another cell.

1950s
British chemist Rosalind Franklin, American biologist James Watson, and British biologist Francis Crick figure out the structure of a DNA (deoxyribonucleic acid) molecule and how it replicates.

For most of human history, people curious about Earth's organisms studied only what they could see with the naked eye. They didn't have the tools to do more. To modern people, this approach might seem awfully limited. But early people managed to discover and figure out many useful things this way. They learned about the abilities and behaviors of the animals they hunted. They found which local plants and animals could be eaten; which ones would make people sick; and which ones could be used for medicine, clothing, or other purposes. People learned about the parts of organisms by examining them during life and after death.

But many aspects of biology simply can't be seen with the naked eye. The processes of disease and reproduction, for example, happen on a tiny scale. Since people couldn't see the steps of these processes happening, they had to make guesses based on what they *could* see.

A depiction of the ancient Greek idea of the human body's four humors: black bile, yellow bile, phlegm, and blood

The ancient Greeks, for instance, explained disease with an idea called humorism. They believed that the human body was made of four humors, or fluids: blood, phlegm, yellow bile, and black bile. When a person's humors were balanced, he or she was healthy. When the humors were out of balance, the person became ill.

The Greeks and other ancient people, such as the Chinese and the Babylonians, explained reproduction—at least partially—with an idea called spontaneous generation. They saw worms emerging from mud, mold growing on bread, mushrooms appearing on trees, and maggots showing up on rotting meat. So people figured that living things could sprout on their own from nonliving material.

MICROSCOPES MAKE THE
INVISIBLE VISIBLE

Before the microscope was invented, people saw living things as whole organisms. They recognized different body parts such as organs and limbs. But they didn't imagine that all these parts were made up of even smaller parts. That view began to change in the 1590s, when father-and-son eyeglass makers Hans and Zacharias Janssen invented the microscope. The Janssens' microscope magnified objects only three to nine times their actual size. But in the 1600s, other scientists tinkered with microscopes to improve their magnification. Before long, the microscopic world became visible to humans.

Dutch eyeglass maker Hans Janssen *(left)* and his son Zacharias invented the first microscope in the late sixteenth century.

In the 1660s, English scholar Robert Hooke designed a lighted microscope. He used it to examine a wide variety of objects and organisms, from mold to fleas to feathers. When he studied thin slices of cork, he was surprised at what he saw:

> I Took a good clear piece of Cork, and . . . cut off . . . an exceeding thin piece of it. . . . I could exceeding plainly perceive it to be all perforated and porous . . . these pores, or cells . . . were indeed the first *microscopical* pores I ever saw, and perhaps, that were ever seen, for I had not met with any Writer or Person, that had made any mention of them before this.

Hooke was the first person to use the word *cell* in the context of biology. He chose this word because the "infinite company of small Boxes" he saw under the microscope reminded him of the cells, or tiny monks'

MICROGRAPHIA'S CRITICS

In 1665 Robert Hooke published his microscopic observations in his best-selling book, *Micrographia*. Many readers found Hooke's observations of insects and other tiny creatures fascinating. But like modern best sellers, *Micrographia* had plenty of critics. Some readers mocked Hooke for paying so much attention to such tiny things—and spending tons of money in the process. Still, Hooke's discoveries provided important background for later biologists.

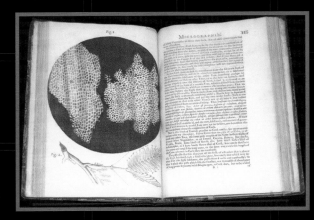

rooms, in a monastery. But Hooke was looking at dead cork. The cells he saw were empty. He had no idea what—if anything—they did.

Antony van Leeuwenhoek, a Dutch businessman, was a highly skilled lens maker who lived around the same time as Hooke. Leeuwenhoek built microscopes that could magnify objects up to 275 times their actual size. In the 1670s, using his powerful microscopes, Leeuwenhoek examined pond water and saliva. He saw "many thousands of living creatures in one small drop of water, all huddling and moving, but each creature having its own motion." He called the creatures "animalcules" (little animals). They were bacteria and other single-celled microbes. Leeuwenhoek had become the first person to see individual living cells under a microscope. But he didn't understand that he was seeing cells. No one made the connection between Hooke's cork cells and Leeuwenhoek's animalcules for about 150 years.

From the late 1600s through the 1700s, scientists generally believed that all living things were made up of some basic unit. But they weren't sure what that unit might be, and they hadn't yet connected this idea with

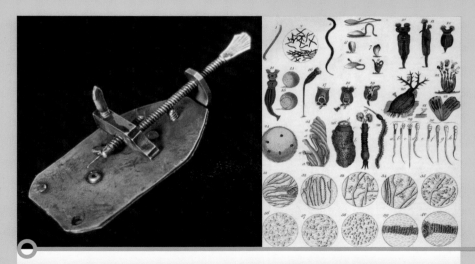

Antony van Leeuwenhoek built a new, stronger microscope *(left)* in the 1670s. Using this tool, he became the first person to see and draw individual living cells, which he called animalcules *(right)*.

Hooke's cells. Many scientists thought that plants and animals were made up of different building blocks: "globules" in plants and "fibers" in animals. Plants' cell walls made their cells, or globules, easily visible. Animal cells, by contrast, had no cell walls and were much harder to see with early microscopes. And animal tissues were fragile; it was hard to prepare slices thin enough for microscopic study.

But biologists were determined to learn more about the building blocks of life. More and more scientists were designing, building, and using microscopes to study organisms. As microscopes improved, scientists could see more details within the microscopic world. By the early 1800s, people began to see similarities between plant cells and animal cells. In 1824 French scientist Henri Dutrochet suggested that animals and plants have a similar cellular structure. He also claimed that cells are not just building blocks but also functional units. In addition to giving things shape, cells carry out the basic processes of life, such as turning food into energy.

So where did these hardworking building blocks come from? Dutrochet and his countryman François Raspail both proposed the important idea that every cell comes from another cell. They were right. But neither scientist understood exactly how new cells formed.

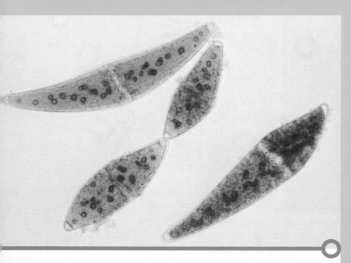

In 1832 Barthelemy Dumortier was the first to see algae cells divide. This discovery helped other scientists understand where new cells come from.

That puzzle was solved by a Belgian scholar, Barthelemy Dumortier. In 1832 Dumortier watched algae cells divide. Each cell formed a partition inside itself, then split into two cells. However, despite the significance of Dumortier's discovery, his work was not well publicized. In fact, German scientist Hugo von Mohl, who observed cell division on his own several years after Dumortier did, is usually incorrectly credited with discovering cell division.

CREATING A **THEORY OF CELLS**

In 1838 and 1839, two German scientists happened to be working at the same laboratory in Berlin, Germany. They were Theodor Schwann, a zoologist, and Matthias Schleiden, a botanist. Schleiden and Schwann used what they had learned from earlier cell scientists, along with their own observations, to establish the first official cell theory. They stated the following:

1. All living organisms are made up of one or more cells.
2. Cells are the basic structural and functional building blocks of all living things.

Schleiden and Schwann believed that living cells formed from nonliving material. But soon other scientists corrected this idea. In 1852 doctor and scientist Robert Remak proved Raspail's idea that all cells arise from preexisting cells. German scholar Rudolf Virchow stole Remak's work and published it as his own. For many years, Virchow mistakenly received credit for Remak's work. But Virchow's dishonest act did, in fact, help spread a better understanding of cell formation. It also completed Schleiden and Schwann's cell theory.

The official cell theory clarified by Schwann, Schleiden, and Remak greatly simplified the way scientists thought about biological puzzles. It provided a framework for understanding reproduction and disease. It replaced incorrect notions of humorism and spontaneous generation.

As microscopes became more powerful in the late 1800s and the early 1900s, scientists gradually discovered the many tiny structures inside cells and learned how these structures work together. For example, in the 1870s, German anatomist Walther Flemming studied wounds and scars, where he found lots of dividing cells. He concluded that the tissues of living things regenerate, or regrow, through cell division. Flemming also studied cells—both tissue cells and reproductive cells—as they divided. He stained the cells with a special dye that allowed him to watch a cell's nucleus during division. He saw that the contents of the nucleus form threadlike structures. These threads then split lengthwise and move to opposite sides of the cell, eventually forming the nuclei of two new cells.

PLAGIARISM AND ANTI-SEMITISM
IN CELL THEORY

Robert Remak, an Orthodox Jew, grew up in Poland and then moved to Berlin to earn his medical degree. When Remak graduated, he tried to get work as a professor, but it was illegal for Jews to teach in Germany at the time. He earned money by working as a medical doctor, and he conducted in-depth research on cells and the nervous system at home in his spare time. For a while, Remak worked for Johannes Müller, who ran the lab in which Schleiden and Schwann had met several years earlier. In his cell research in Müller's lab, Remak watched cells divide and multiply and suggested that all cells come from other cells. But when he published his work, people didn't believe him. Even Müller, his own supervisor, failed to support him. Remak's colleague Rudolf Virchow was eventually convinced, but instead of crediting Remak, Virchow used his own excellent reputation as a professor and a Christian to pass Remak's ideas off as his own.

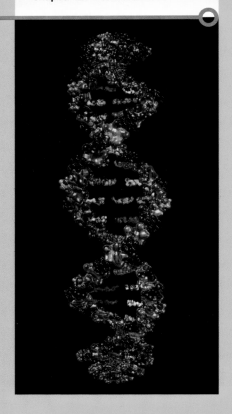

In the 1950s, Rosalind Franklin, James Watson, and Francis Crick figured out the structure of a DNA molecule, which is shaped like a twisted ladder.

Flemming's studies helped later scientists realize that cells must divide for organisms to grow, heal, and reproduce. And for cells to divide, the original, or parent, cells must contain hereditary information, which they pass on to new, or daughter, cells. This hereditary information lies in the DNA molecules that make up the threadlike chromosomes found in the nucleus of every cell. When a cell divides, its DNA is copied for each daughter cell to use. In the decades after Flemming's discoveries, several other scientists made further breakthroughs in the study of heredity through DNA.

In the 1950s, British chemist Rosalind Franklin, American biologist James Watson, and British biologist Francis Crick figured out the structure of a DNA molecule and how it copies itself. They concluded that the molecule is shaped like a twisted ladder. It reproduces by "unzipping," or splitting apart, to form two parent strands, which each then pick up the chemicals they need to complete themselves and form two new daughter molecules.

After these discoveries, scientists adapted the original cell theory to include a few more key ideas. These changes established modern cell theory, which states the following:

1. Cells make up all living things.
2. Cells are the functional and structural building blocks of all organisms.
3. All cells come from existing cells. They form through the process of cell division.
4. Cells contain hereditary information. Parent cells pass this information to daughter cells during cell division.

5. The same basic chemicals compose all cells.
6. All energy transfer in living things happens inside their cells.

Cell theory is one of the most important concepts in biology. It provides a consistent way of understanding, explaining, and learning more about all living things. But there's one important aspect of biology that cell theory doesn't address: how the first cell formed. Most scientists believe that this must have happened over an extremely long time, in a series of gradual steps in which nonliving chemicals developed and joined to form living cells. Ironically, that would be an example of spontaneous generation—which cell theory says cannot happen!

STUDYING **STEM CELLS**

Modern biologists of all kinds agree on at least one thing: early in development, all organisms start out with stem cells, which develop into many kinds of mature, specialized cells. Until recently, scientists believed that this was a one-way trip—a mature cell, such as a skin cell, could not revert into a stem cell.

A Japanese scientist named Shinya Yamanaka disproved this idea in 2006. He discovered that it took only four genes, or segments of DNA, to make mature cells turn back into stem cells. Stem cells are in high demand because scientists worldwide use them to develop treatments for human diseases such as diabetes and heart failure. Unfortunately, Yamanaka's method uses a virus to insert genes into a cell, which raises the risk of cancer. Scientists are still searching for simpler and safer methods.

Shinya Yamanaka won the Nobel Prize in 2012 for his years of research on stem cells.

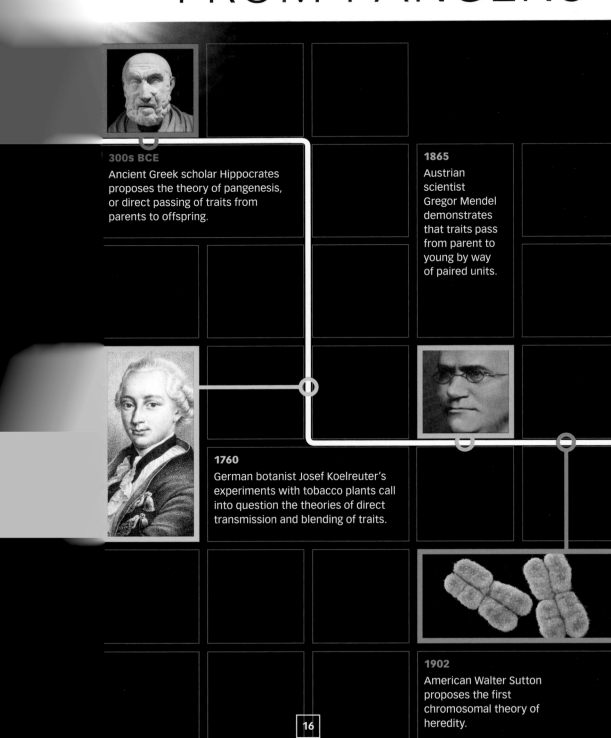

300s BCE
Ancient Greek scholar Hippocrates proposes the theory of pangenesis, or direct passing of traits from parents to offspring.

1865
Austrian scientist Gregor Mendel demonstrates that traits pass from parent to young by way of paired units.

1760
German botanist Josef Koelreuter's experiments with tobacco plants call into question the theories of direct transmission and blending of traits.

1902
American Walter Sutton proposes the first chromosomal theory of heredity.

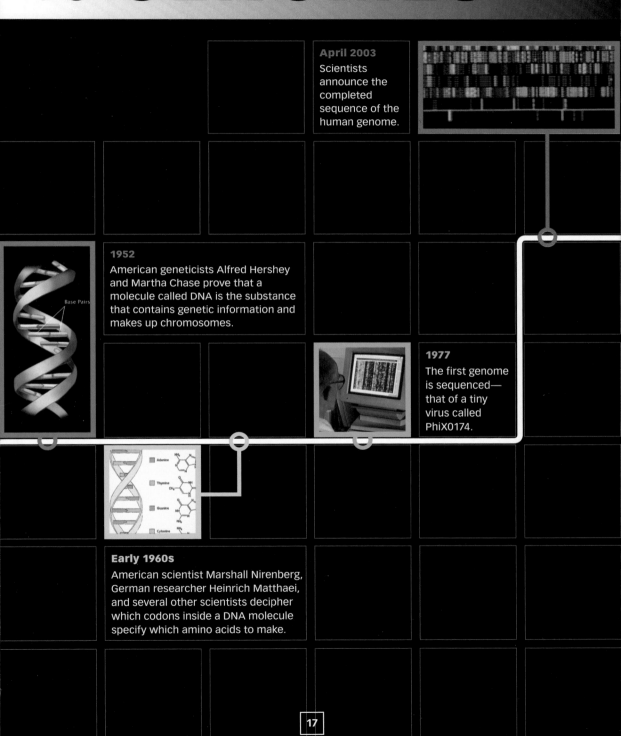

April 2003
Scientists announce the completed sequence of the human genome.

1952
American geneticists Alfred Hershey and Martha Chase prove that a molecule called DNA is the substance that contains genetic information and makes up chromosomes.

Base Pairs

1977
The first genome is sequenced—that of a tiny virus called PhiX0174.

Adenine

Thymine

Guanine

Cytosine

Early 1960s
American scientist Marshall Nirenberg, German researcher Heinrich Matthaei, and several other scientists decipher which codons inside a DNA molecule specify which amino acids to make.

Scientists believed in spontaneous generation for a long time. That may seem outrageous to modern people. But it's important to realize that spontaneous generation was just one way humans explained the appearance of new organisms. They knew about other ways too. They knew that many plants reproduce via seeds. They knew that animals mate and have babies.

People also noticed the patterns that happened during reproduction. They saw that plants and animals passed certain traits on to their young. Farmers managed to control many of the traits their animals and plants passed on to future generations. Because certain breeds of sheep provided better wool and meat, for instance, farmers made efforts to allow those breeds to reproduce. So people knew about heredity, the passing on of traits from parents to young. But no one truly understood how it worked.

They definitely had ideas, though. The ancient Greek scholar Hippocrates believed that particles called pangens came together from all parts of the body to form what were later called eggs and sperm. The eggs and sperm then joined to produce offspring. So, for example, Hippocrates thought that if a father had an unusually shaped limb, his sperm would contain material from that limb. The material would pass directly to his child and produce the same kind of limb in the child. Hippocrates's theory,

THE **CAMELEOPARD**

For many centuries, people believed not only in direct transmission and blending but also that very different species could mate and have offspring that were bizarre mixtures of both animals. The giraffe is a good example of this belief. People thought that giraffes were the offspring of camels and leopards. The giraffe's scientific name, *Giraffa camelopardalis*, is evidence of this belief.

Humans are very physically diverse, even after many generations of reproduction. This disproves the once-accepted theory that the traits of one parent blend with the traits of the other to produce young.

called pangenesis, or direct transmission of traits, was widely accepted by scientists. People didn't begin to question it until the late 1700s.

Around then the blending theory of heredity was popular. The blending theory relied on the theory of direct transmission. This idea suggested that parents' traits blend to form the traits of the young. According to this theory, a black dog mating with a white dog would have a gray puppy. A tall man and a short woman would have a child of medium height. Many observations seemed to support this idea. But the blending theory couldn't explain how two brown-eyed parents could have a blue-eyed baby. Nor could it explain why one offspring of a pair of parents might look like the mother, while another offspring of the same parents might resemble the father.

The blending theory raised another puzzling question too. If parental traits blend in every generation of offspring, eventually all the members of a species should have the same physical traits. They should look the same and have the same abilities. But this clearly doesn't happen. Within most species, individuals differ quite a bit. Humans, for example, have existed for tens of thousands of years. Yet even after such a long history on Earth, people are physically diverse. They come in a variety of shapes, sizes, and colors, with a wide range of characteristics and abilities.

When botanist Josef Koelreuter experimented with breeding tobacco plants, he learned that genetic traits can skip a generation.

In the late 1700s, scientists began to poke holes in the heredity theories of direct transmission and blending. In 1760 German botanist Josef Koelreuter did a series of experiments with tobacco plants. He bred different strains of tobacco (the first generation) and ended up with offspring (the second generation) that could reproduce. These offspring looked different from both parents. When Koelreuter bred the offspring, *their* offspring (the third generation) varied a lot in appearance. Some of the third-generation offspring resembled their parents (the second generation), but a few resembled their grandparents (the first generation). Koelreuter's experiments showed that traits could be masked in one generation, only to reappear in the next. Traits didn't blend, and they weren't passed on directly.

Over the next century, other scientists expanded on Koelreuter's work. They performed similar experiments with different plants, and they got similar results. It was becoming obvious that direct transmission and blending were not happening. But in those days, scientists rarely recorded exact numbers in their results. So it was hard to analyze the results to figure out what *was* happening.

GREGOR MENDEL'S **GENE THEORY**

In 1865 Austrian scientist Gregor Mendel set out to learn more about how traits pass from one generation to the next. He performed breeding experiments with pea plants, and unlike the scientists before him, he carefully recorded his results. Working with recorded data allowed Mendel to understand how traits were passed on. For instance, Mendel bred a plant with yellow peas and a plant with green peas. All the young plants had yellow peas. When Mendel bred two of the offspring, one-quarter of *their* offspring had green peas. Mendel decided that the factors that cause different traits, such as pea color, must happen in paired units. Modern scientists call these units genes. One unit is recessive, or weaker. The other is dominant, or stronger. When a dominant unit is paired with a recessive one, it hides the recessive unit.

Mendel published the results of his experiments, but the world didn't pay much attention to them. It wasn't until 1900 that three scientists, independently searching the scientific literature before publishing the results of their own heredity experiments, rediscovered Mendel's work. These three were Dutch botanist Hugo de Vries, German botanist Carl Correns, and Austrian botanist Erich von Tschermak. After this rediscovery, many scientists tested Mendel's ideas.

By the late 1800s, microscopes had become powerful enough for people to see the parts that made up cells. Scientists saw tiny rod-shaped or threadlike objects inside cells and called them chromosomes. However, scientists did not know what chromosomes were made of or what they did. It wasn't until the early 1900s that scientists who were studying dividing cells realized what they were seeing. They noticed that similar

In the 1860s, Gregor Mendel *(top)* learned from breeding pea plants that traits pass down in paired units, later called genes. Decades later, scientists figured out that chromosomes *(bottom)* contain genes.

In the early 1900s, Walter Sutton proposed that chromosomes were the paired genetic units Mendel had referred to. In 1953 James Watson and Francis Crick figured out the structure of DNA *(below)*.

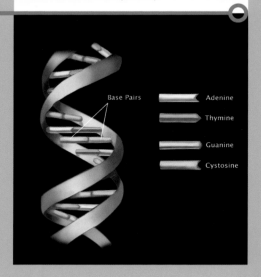

Base Pairs

Adenine

Thymine

Guanine

Cystosine

chromosomes paired up during cell division. Scientists realized these must have something to do with the paired units that Mendel had theorized. They determined that chromosomes were responsible for passing on traits, and therefore, chromosomes must contain genes. In 1902 American Walter Sutton became the first to put this discovery into words. His chromosomal theory of heredity stated that the pairing and dividing of chromosomes was proof that Mendel's ideas about how parents pass on traits were correct. Chromosomes contained the paired units that Mendel had discussed. Chromosomes were responsible for heredity.

DECIPHERING THE **MYSTERIES OF DNA**

In the 1940s and the 1950s, Canadian American biologist Oswald Avery and American geneticists Alfred Hershey and Martha Chase pushed the work of Mendel and Sutton even further. They proved that chromosomes are made of molecules called deoxyribonucleic acid. It was DNA that contained the genetic information that passed on traits. Scientists knew that DNA was made up of an acid called phosphate; a sugar called deoxyribose; and four chemical bases called nucleotides: adenine (A), cytosine (C), guanine (G), and thymine (T). But scientists didn't know how these pieces fit together.

American biologist James Watson and British biologist Francis Crick figured out the structure of DNA just one year later, in 1953. A friend of Watson's showed him an X-ray image of DNA that British chemist Rosalind Franklin had made two years earlier. Watson and Crick could tell that the DNA molecule was shaped like a twisted ladder. Using their knowledge of nucleotide structure, they deduced that the sides of the ladder are chains of phosphate and deoxyribose. The rungs of the ladder are the nucleotides. The nucleotides always pair up. C always binds to G, and A always binds to T.

Scientists had long suspected that genes (contained in DNA) and proteins were somehow related. They knew that proteins were responsible for the activities that happen inside cells. Proteins are chains of molecules called amino acids. The order of amino acids in the chain determines the job that protein does. The jobs of proteins are to carry out the chemical processes that maintain life, such as turning food into energy and reproducing. Proteins are also responsible for a living thing's physical traits, or how it behaves and looks. Watson and Crick reasoned that the order of nucleotides in DNA must work as a code that gives protein-making instructions.

Crick and three other researchers, Leslie Barnett, Sydney Brenner, and Richard Watts-Tobin, figured out how that code works in 1961. They explained that three nucleotides in a row make up a codon. Some codons say which amino acid to make. Others start or stop the process of making amino acids. Amino acids join to form proteins, which then carry out the work of the cell.

Later in 1961, American scientist Marshall Nirenberg and German Heinrich Matthaei figured out which amino acid was specified by one

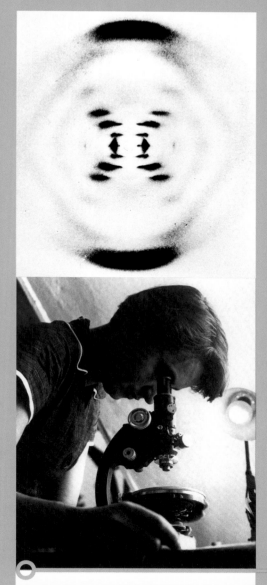

This X-ray photograph of DNA *(top)* was a key tool that James Watson and Frances Crick used to figure out the structure of a DNA molecule. The X-ray was created by British chemist Rosalind Franklin *(bottom)*.

particular codon. Over the next few years, Nirenberg and several other scientists deciphered the rest of the genetic code. They described which codons specify which amino acids. The code is the same in all organisms, from potatoes to people.

Throughout the 1950s, the 1960s, and the 1970s, many scientists took apart cells to figure out how DNA copied itself and how proteins formed. Scientists also developed technologies that helped them see and tinker with specific segments of DNA. These discoveries set the stage for scientists to sequence an entire genome in 1977. An organism's genome is all the DNA in that organism. Sequencing is figuring out the exact order of the nucleotides in the organism's DNA. The first genome sequenced was that of a tiny virus called PhiX0174. After that, scientists sequenced more genomes: a bacterium in 1995, a roundworm

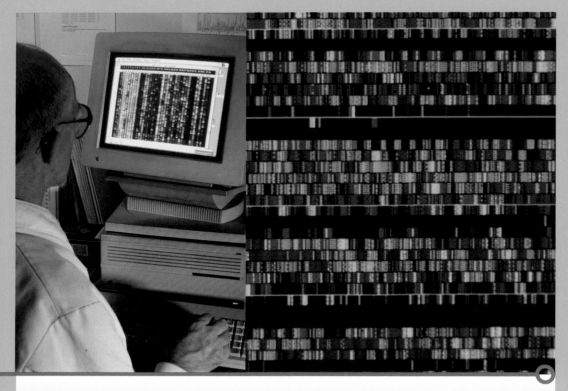

A geneticist uses a computer to sequence an organism's DNA *(left)*. A human DNA sequence *(right)* looks like a series of brightly colored bars. The colors represent different nucleotides. Sequencing allows scientists to see which genes are responsible for different tasks.

in 1998, the fruit fly in 1999, and the human genome in April 2003. The sequencing of the human genome had taken thousands of researchers at hundreds of laboratories around the world a whopping thirteen years to complete.

Why did scientists want to sequence genomes, anyway? An organism's genome shows how it resembles and differs from other organisms. It also shows how individuals within a species resemble and differ from one another. A sequenced genome helps scientists understand how an organism's body works. It can also help scientists and doctors diagnose, prevent, and treat some diseases.

Knowledge of the human genome has already led to the discovery of more than eighteen hundred genes connected to disease. More than two thousand tests for human genetic conditions are available. It once took years for scientists to find a gene suspected of causing a disease. But modern researchers can find a gene within days. With such tools at hand, doctors can analyze patients' risk of disease and diagnose genetic conditions more quickly and accurately. They can also use genetic tests to recommend the most effective treatments. For example, they can tell whether a breast cancer patient's body will respond to the drug Herceptin or figure out the right dose of the blood-thinning drug Warfarin for a patient with heart disease.

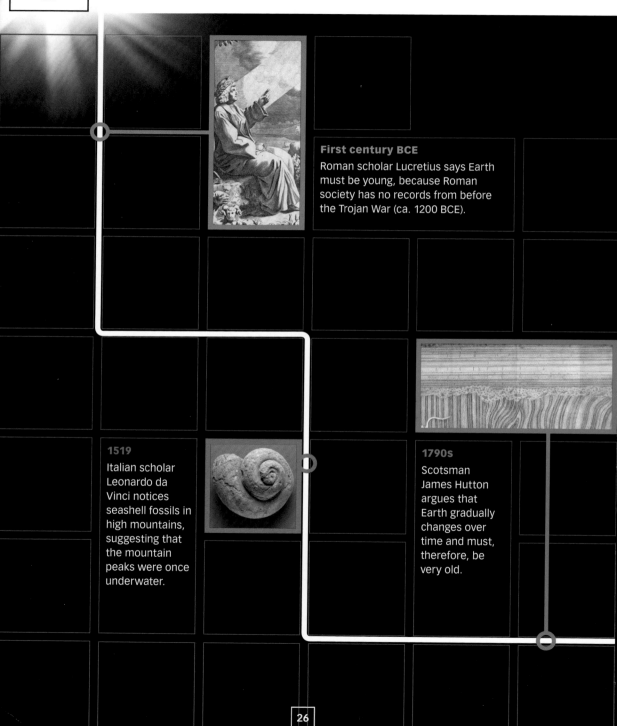

First century BCE
Roman scholar Lucretius says Earth must be young, because Roman society has no records from before the Trojan War (ca. 1200 BCE).

1519
Italian scholar Leonardo da Vinci notices seashell fossils in high mountains, suggesting that the mountain peaks were once underwater.

1790s
Scotsman James Hutton argues that Earth gradually changes over time and must, therefore, be very old.

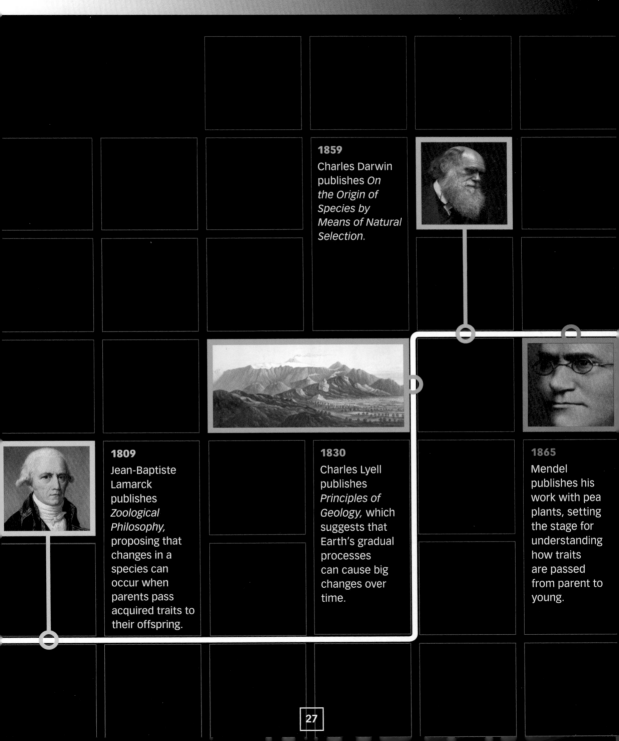

1859

Charles Darwin publishes *On the Origin of Species by Means of Natural Selection.*

1809

Jean-Baptiste Lamarck publishes *Zoological Philosophy,* proposing that changes in a species can occur when parents pass acquired traits to their offspring.

1830

Charles Lyell publishes *Principles of Geology,* which suggests that Earth's gradual processes can cause big changes over time.

1865

Mendel publishes his work with pea plants, setting the stage for understanding how traits are passed from parent to young.

Before the 1800s, most people thought that Earth was just a few thousand years old. They believed that all the organisms on Earth had been created along with Earth. They also believed that living things had stayed more or less unchanged since then. There were exceptions, of course. But this widely held idea went back at least two thousand years. The Roman scholar Lucretius, who lived in the first century BCE, believed Earth must be young because Roman society had no records older than the Trojan War, which historians believe happened around 1200 BCE.

The belief in a young Earth with unchanging inhabitants strengthened during the Middle Ages, when religion strongly influenced scientific thought in Europe and the Middle East. Many scholars in this region believed Earth had been peopled since its beginning. They thought they could figure out Earth's age by calculating how long humans had lived on Earth. They studied all the ancient human records they could find, including the Jewish Torah, the Christian Bible, and the Muslim Quran. Scholars decided Earth was only a few millennia old—anywhere from about four thousand to ten thousand years.

AN OLD AND **EVER-CHANGING EARTH**

It wasn't until the 1500s that scientists began to question this belief. They realized that Earth must have undergone many processes that took longer than a few millennia. In the early 1500s, for instance, Italian scholar Leonardo da Vinci noticed fossils of seashells high in the mountains. That made him wonder if the mountains had been underwater at one time. In the 1790s, Scotsman James Hutton argued that Earth transformed by slow changes such as erosion and sedimentation. These processes are so gradual that humans don't really notice them. But over a long time, they can produce big changes. In the early 1800s, other geologists collected evidence that supported Hutton's idea, which became known as uniformitarianism. One supporter, Englishman Charles Lyell, published a book titled *Principles of Geology* in 1830. This book spread the notion of uniformitarianism far and wide.

ETERNAL EARTH

The revered Greek thinker Aristotle (300s BCE) was one of the few scholars in his part of the world who opposed the idea of a young Earth. He thought Earth had always existed and was infinitely old. The Hindu scholars of ancient India (500 BCE to 500 CE) had a different concept of an eternal Earth. They said that every 4.32 billion years, the universe explodes, expands, collapses, and starts over *(right)*. They believed the last big bang had happened 1.97 billion years ago and that the next big crunch would happen in 2.35 billion years.

Meanwhile, other scientists were questioning the belief that each species of a living thing had always been the same. French botanist Jean-Baptiste Lamarck was one of the first scientists who dared to put this idea in writing. As he studied fossils of shellfish, spiders, worms, and other invertebrates, the evidence he saw convinced him that a species can change over time. In 1809 Lamarck published a book titled *Zoological Philosophy*. In it he suggested that as a living thing's habitat changes, the organism changes its behavior to survive. For example, if an individual organism uses a certain body part more, that part gradually grows stronger and bigger. If an individual uses a body part less, that part gradually weakens and shrinks. Lamarck also said that an individual can pass on such body changes to its young. As a result, a species changes continually as its members adapt to their habitats.

Lamarck's peers thought his ideas were ridiculous—mainly because they didn't accept the idea of change in species. And modern scientists know that Lamarck's explanation of *how* species change was all wrong. Many traits, such as strong muscles, can only be acquired during life. They cannot be passed from parents to offspring. But Lamarck's work was important anyway. It opened the door for discussion about evolution, or the idea that species can change over time.

Lamarck's and Lyell's books both made big impressions on English naturalist Charles Darwin. Darwin read Lyell's book while taking a sea voyage around the world. *Principles of Geology* enabled Darwin to see the places he visited—and their inhabitants—through the lens of deep history.

At the age of twenty-two, Darwin took a job as naturalist for a five-year scientific expedition on a ship called the *Beagle*. The *Beagle* left Plymouth, England, in 1831 and sailed westward around the world before returning home in 1836. As he traveled, Darwin studied plants, animals, fossils, and landforms that most European scientists had never seen. He

Jean-Baptiste Lamarck *(left)* was one of the earliest scientists to suggest that organisms change over time in response to their environment. Around the same time, Charles Lyell published evidence that Earth itself changes over time in response to erosion and sedimentation *(right)*.

Charles Darwin spent five years traveling on the *Beagle*, studying organisms and landforms around the world.

collected and analyzed many samples of plants and animals. He also kept a detailed journal. Here's what he noticed:

- Rock formations and fossil locations suggested that continents and oceans had changed a lot over time.
- Sedimentary rocks suggested that Earth and its inhabitants had changed gradually.
- Variations among different populations of the same species on island chains suggested that species do change.

Seeing tropical rain forests and unfamiliar species encouraged Darwin to ponder why life is so diverse. And native cultures dramatically different from the European cultures Darwin was familiar with made him wonder how civilizations develop. He also wondered about the relationships between humans and other animals.

Darwin took more than twenty years to think about what he'd seen and what it meant. He probably would have taken even longer if a colleague, Alfred Russel Wallace, had not written to him in 1858. Wallace

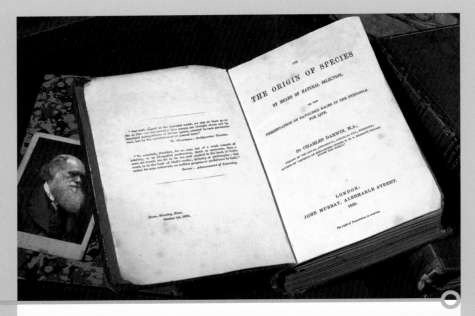

In 1859 Charles Darwin *(left)* published his book *On the Origin of Species by Means of Natural Selection,* which proposed his theory of natural selection.

wrote about a theory that was nearly identical to the one Darwin himself was developing. Wallace and Darwin agreed to present their ideas jointly to the scientific community. One year later, Darwin published his book *On the Origin of Species by Means of Natural Selection, or the Preservation of Favoured Races in the Struggle for Life.*

DARWIN'S THEORY OF **EVOLUTION**

In his book, Darwin proposed that individual members of a species that happen to be well suited to their habitats are more likely to survive and reproduce than individuals less suited to their habitats. This process is called natural selection. Darwin's theory includes the following:

1. Members of the same species have variations in their physical traits. This occurs by chance.
2. Any given population of a species tends to produce more young than its habitat can support.

3. All members of the population in a habitat compete with one another for the available resources. The members struggle to survive.
4. The organisms that survive pass on their desirable traits to their young.
5. Over time, habitats change. When this happens, different traits become desirable.
6. As nature "selects" new traits, the population of a species starts to be different from the original population.
7. The individuals of the population eventually grow so different from the original individuals that the population becomes a new species.

Darwin did not know why or how physical traits vary within a species. But he was convinced that such variations existed and that parents passed such variations along to their offspring.

Just a few years after the publication of *On the Origin of Species by Means of Natural Selection*, Gregor Mendel did his pea plant experiments. Mendel's work set science on the road to understanding heredity. Several decades later, as the result of many scientists' work, people realized that genes contained in DNA determine all physical traits.

Mutations—sudden, spontaneous changes in the chemical building blocks of genes—are the key to variation within a species. When cells divide, errors in copying can produce daughter DNA that's a bit different from the parent DNA. Most mutations are neutral; they neither help nor harm the organism. Some mutations create traits that are not very well suited to the organism's habitat. Some create traits that are better suited to the habitat. Mutations can pass from parent to young. As time goes by, the number of individuals in a population that have a certain mutation may grow. Later, if the habitat changes in some way, mutations that were not helpful earlier may turn out to be helpful. Individuals carrying such mutations may have a better chance of surviving than other individuals of their species have.

When Charles Darwin introduced the theory of evolution by natural selection more than 150 years ago, his peers argued over it fiercely. This was no surprise. The concept challenged many dearly held religious and cultural ideas. But over time, evidence from the fields of genetics, molecular biology, paleontology, and zoology gradually established the truth of evolution. Scientists continue to argue over the minute

The bird-dinosaur *Archaeopteryx* is an example of a transitional species, or one that has characteristics of an earlier species combined with those of a later species. This image is a scientist's guess about how *Archaeopteryx* looked.

details of how, exactly, evolution works. But no real debate exists in the scientific community over whether evolution by natural selection actually occurs.

TRANSITIONAL **FISH**

Paleontologists have discovered many examples of fossils that represent a transition between two species. For example, *Archaeopteryx* combines feathers and bone structures of birds with dinosaur features such as a full set of teeth; a flat breastbone; a long, bony tail; belly ribs; and three claws on each wing. In another example of transition, four-legged animals that walked on land were the ancestors of modern whales, and fossils show that animals called *Ambulocetus* and *Rodhocetus* helped make that shift.

EVOLUTION **IN EDUCATION**

Outside the scientific community—and especially in the United States—some people are still arguing against evolution. That's because it seems to contradict the biblical creation story of Judaism and Christianity and it challenges the idea of a god who actively guides and cares for creation. Though most Jews and Christians do not believe in a literal interpretation of the creation story, those who do are very vocal. The most intense debate centers on what public schoolchildren should be taught about the origin and development of life. In some schools, districts, and states, opponents of evolution have tried to establish policies requiring disclaimers about evolution or requiring the teaching of alternative theories with biblical foundations. But so far, federal courts have found all these efforts to be government promotion of a specific religion, which

In 2014 researchers discovered a fossil of a fish called *Tiktaalik*, which had characteristics of legs. This transitional fish lived about 375 million years ago.

Another important transition in the history of life on Earth happened even earlier. At first, all of Earth's creatures lived in the water. But eventually life moved onto land as well. Scientists call the first creatures to leave the water tetrapods. Tetrapods are the ancestors of all modern amphibians, birds, mammals, and reptiles.

Scientists have known for a long time that tetrapods evolved from fish with fleshy fins. One famous example of this kind of fish is the coelacanth. But until recently, scientists had no evidence to show when fleshy fins began to evolve into bony limbs. Then, in 2004, researchers discovered a fossil fish called *Tiktaalik* in Arctic Canada. *Tiktaalik* was a fish, but it had the beginnings of toes, wrists, elbows, and shoulders. This creature lived about 375 million years ago.

4 WEAVING THE WEB

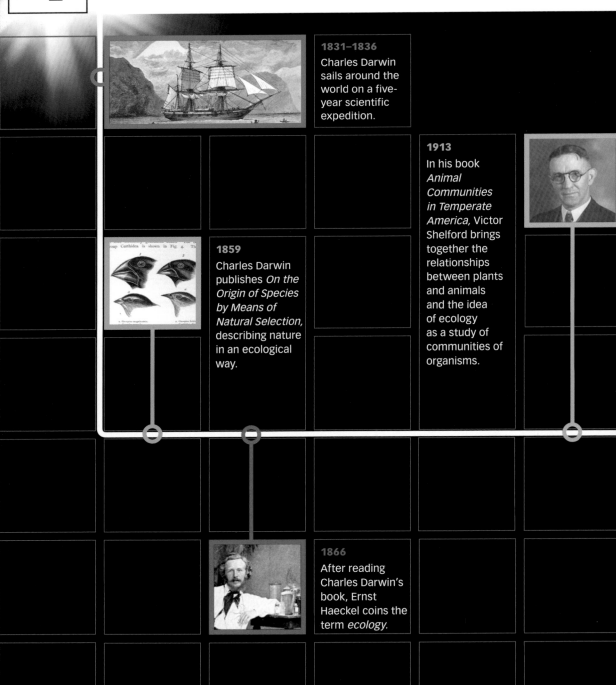

1831–1836
Charles Darwin sails around the world on a five-year scientific expedition.

1859
Charles Darwin publishes *On the Origin of Species by Means of Natural Selection,* describing nature in an ecological way.

1913
In his book *Animal Communities in Temperate America,* Victor Shelford brings together the relationships between plants and animals and the idea of ecology as a study of communities of organisms.

1866
After reading Charles Darwin's book, Ernst Haeckel coins the term *ecology.*

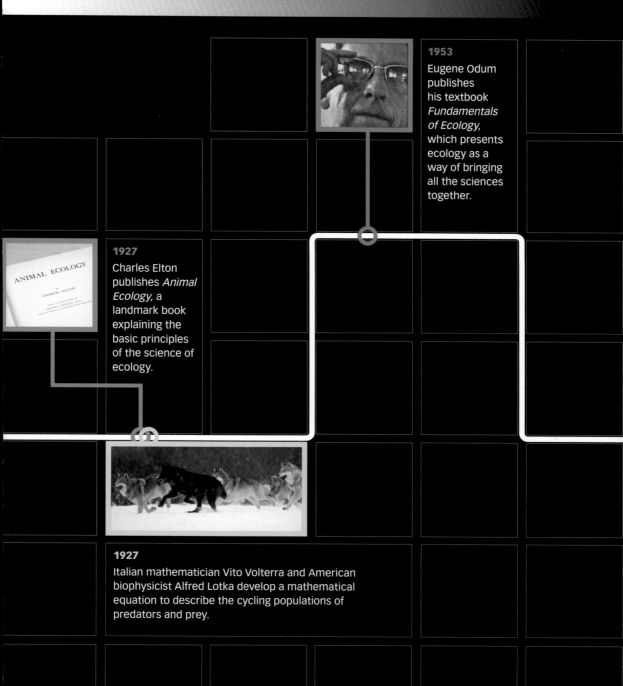

1953

Eugene Odum publishes his textbook *Fundamentals of Ecology,* which presents ecology as a way of bringing all the sciences together.

1927

Charles Elton publishes *Animal Ecology,* a landmark book explaining the basic principles of the science of ecology.

1927

Italian mathematician Vito Volterra and American biophysicist Alfred Lotka develop a mathematical equation to describe the cycling populations of predators and prey.

Modern people frequently hear the word *ecology* and its many offshoots, such as *eco-friendly* and *eco-conscious*. The environment on Earth is changing dramatically and rapidly, and humans are scrambling to cope with those changes. Many people know that Earth and all its inhabitants influence and are influenced by one another. Not long ago, though, interest in this concept was rare—and radical.

Ecology is the study of how organisms interact with one another and the environment. It is a science that integrates all human knowledge about life on Earth, including chemistry, climatology, economics, genetics, geography, geology, physics, physiology, sociology, and more. Scientists have been studying specific organisms and environments for thousands of years. But they didn't really start thinking about all these habitats and their inhabitants as systems until the 1800s.

A NEW WAY **OF THINKING**

Many historians credit Charles Darwin with introducing the concept of ecology. The word *ecology* didn't exist when Darwin sailed around the world on the *Beagle* from 1831 to 1836. And he didn't invent this term or use it in any of his writings. But he clearly was observing nature in a new, ecological way. He saw how the places, people, plants, and creatures on his journey were intertwined. He spotted patterns of life in particular habitats and explained them with his theory of evolution by natural selection. This theory approaches nature as a system in which all parts, both living and nonliving, affect one another.

The word *ecology* came later, from German biologist and doctor Ernst Haeckel. In 1859, after reading Darwin's *On the Origin of Species by Means of Natural Selection,* Haeckel quit his medical practice and turned his attention to scientific research. His studies of invertebrates led him to new ideas about animal development. Unlike Darwin, Haeckel believed that the environment acts directly on organisms, producing new races, or groups within species (a version of Lamarck's incorrect theory). He said that this is how the survival of a race depends on its interaction with the environment. He coined the term *oekologie* to mean the relationship of

THINKING ECOLOGICALLY:
DARWIN'S FINCHES

During Darwin's journey on the *Beagle*, he studied finches. His observations of these birds helped him form his theory of evolution by natural selection. Darwin suspected that the finch species he'd seen in the Galápagos Islands were close relatives of one another and of a species of finches that he'd seen in South America. The finches all looked similar. But each species had physical traits tailored to its environment. For example, beak shape differed based on feeding methods. Finches that ate seeds on the ground had differently shaped beaks than finches that ate berries in trees. Darwin reasoned that all the finches on the islands had descended from the species on the mainland of Central or South America. He thought the finches' bodies had, over a very long time, adapted to the different kinds of food available wherever they settled. Darwin's reasoning shows that he was thinking in ecological terms.

animals with their environment, including both the living and nonliving parts of that environment. Haeckel's term comes from the Greek word *oikos*, which means "home."

Despite ecology's whole-system approach, plant ecology and animal ecology were once two separate fields of study. The different camps often disagreed with or ignored each other. American zoologist Victor Shelford was the first to point out the importance of plant-animal relationships and to look at ecology as the study of communities of living things. His 1913 book *Animal Communities in Temperate America* was one of the first books to treat ecology as a science unto itself.

Ernst Haeckel *(left)*, shown here with his assistant, coined the German term *oekologie*, which we know as *ecology* in English.

English zoologist Charles Elton read and admired Shelford's ideas. In the 1920s, Elton made four expeditions to the Arctic to study the communities of animals and plants living there. Elton then published a book titled *Animal Ecology* in 1927. This book became a landmark in ecology because

FOOD **CHAINS**

A food chain is a sequence of living things arranged according to what they eat. Each organism in a food chain gets nutrients from the organism that comes before it and in turn passes on nutrients to the next organism. Sunlight is the first link in nearly every food chain on Earth.

For example, a tomato plant absorbs sunlight. The plant also takes in carbon dioxide and water from the soil and air. The sunlight's energy sparks a chemical reaction in the plant. The carbon dioxide and water molecules break up. They rearrange into oxygen and sugar molecules. The plant releases the oxygen into the air. It uses the sugar as food to grow and function.

The molecules that make up the tomato plant contain chemical energy. Eventually another living thing uses that energy. A herbivore, such as a squirrel, might eat the tomato. The squirrel digests the tomato. Chemicals in the squirrel's body react with the chemicals in the tomato. This breaks down the tomato's molecular bonds and releases energy. The squirrel uses that energy to move and grow.

A carnivore, such as a coyote, might then eat the squirrel, supplying energy to the coyote. Or the squirrel might simply die. Then the squirrel's body becomes food for decomposers. Decomposers are living organisms that feed on dead organisms as well as waste (feces) produced by both plant eaters and meat eaters. Many bacteria, fungi, and small animals are decomposers. They return nutrients back to the earth. They make those nutrients available for more plants to use.

the main ideas of his discussion became the basic principles of ecology as a science. Elton said that different animal populations form communities within their habitat. He introduced the idea of an ecological niche. That's the idea that each species has a unique job within its habitat. He noted that a certain quantity of plants must supply food for a smaller quantity of plant-eating animals. The plant-eating animals then provide food for an even smaller quantity of meat-eating animals. Elton called this network of food relationships a pyramid of numbers.

Around the same time, scientists began applying the principles of ecology to environmental problems. Italian mathematician Vito Volterra and American biophysicist Alfred Lotka independently developed a mathematical way to describe the rising and falling populations of predators and prey. Although Volterra and Lotka didn't work together, they both came up with the same equation. As a result, the equation, the Lotka-Volterra prey-predator model, is named after both of them. The 1927 model shows that growth of the prey population causes growth of the predator population. Growth of the predator population then leads to a decline in the prey. That decline, in turn, leads to a decline in the predator population. Volterra's and Lotka's work turned out to be important not only as an approach to environmental problems but also because it was the first use of complex mathematics in ecology.

MODERN ECOLOGY

In the early 1900s, most people—including most scientists—thought that ecology was a trivial branch of biology. They believed the job of ecologists was to observe, describe, and classify species. But Eugene Odum, a professor of zoology at the University of Georgia, argued that ecology wasn't a branch of anything. Rather, he said, it was a complex academic discipline that integrated all the sciences. He promoted this idea through his teaching and writing from 1940 until his death in 2002. His 1953 textbook *Fundamentals of Ecology* was the first of its kind. For these efforts, Odum became known as the father of modern ecology. Among many other things, he pointed out that "in nature, there are a lot of answers about what we should be doing in society. Nature has been here longer than humans and survived a lot of catastrophes."

Modern ecologists continue to build upon Odum's vision. They use the latest technology to explore nature. Among the most important tools modern ecologists have are geographic information systems (GIS). GIS is any computer system that captures, checks, displays, or stores information about locations on Earth's surface. GIS can show many different kinds of data on one map. This helps people compare the locations of different things and discover how they relate to one another. GIS also helps researchers look at change over time.

GIS can, for example, help ecologists track vegetation change through time and make predictions about future vegetation change. A researcher can use satellite data to study how much of the polar regions is covered in ice at different times. Biologists can use GIS to track animal migration patterns or population changes. A scientist could use GIS to create a map showing sites that produce pollution, such as factories, and sites that are sensitive to pollution, such as wetlands, to figure out which wetlands have the highest risk of being polluted. With this technology and the information it gathers, ecologists hope to keep learning more about the living organisms on Earth.

Eugene Odum *(top),* known as the father of modern ecology, argued that ecology was an academic discipline that incorporated all branches of science. Modern ecologists build upon Odum's vision with tools such as GIS *(bottom),* which can show different kinds of data about Earth on one map.

A PERSISTENT **PUZZLE**

The development of cell theory, genetics, the theory of evolution by natural selection, and ecology make up just four of countless chapters in the story of biology. But these chapters illustrate some important truths about all life sciences. The same truths apply no matter what puzzles biologists are trying to solve about which organisms.

- All organisms consist of one or more cells. These cells are made of the same basic chemicals and function in the same way in all living things.
- All living things respond to their environments. They sense what is going on around them. They react when the environment changes. They grow and change.
- All organisms reproduce. They make more organisms like themselves. And all living things pass their traits on to their offspring via DNA.
- Despite the basic similarities among all living things, variations exist. Species differ from one another. So do separate populations of the same species and individuals within a population. All species change through evolution by natural selection.
- All living things affect and are affected by other living things.

Although biologists have learned a lot about the business of life on Earth over the past few millennia, the story of biology is far from over. It is as old as humankind, and it will go on as long as humans do.

New discoveries in biology—about everything from cells to genomes to ecosystems—make the potential for future discoveries seem limitless. But it's important to remember that life science discoveries don't happen on their own. Every new discovery or theory is part of a much larger structure of ideas. Every new idea is built upon a foundation that reaches deep into history. Key events on the timeline of biology happen because of all the events that happened before them.

YOUR TURN ON THE TIMELINE

Milestones in life science are not just a list of dates. They are events that affect people's day-to-day lives. Use what you have learned in this book, along with your creativity and writing skills, to compose a short letter to someone close to you.

First, choose an event listed on one of the timelines in this book. Next, picture yourself as a scientist involved with that event. Imagine what it felt like to make that breakthrough, and use your letter to tell your friend or family member all about your experience. Were you surprised? What effects will this new knowledge or discovery have on your life? What will it mean for your family, friends, and colleagues? Can you predict how your world will be different?

After writing your letter, jump online or head to your local library. Can you find any letters that scientists wrote about the milestone you chose? How do they compare to *your* letter?

LERNER

SOURCE™

Expand learning beyond the printed book. Download free, complementary educational resources for this book from our website, www.lerneresource.com.

SOURCE NOTES

9 Fiona Barnard, "Micrographia," *University of Reading Special Collections*, March 2008, accessed May 27, 2014, https://www.reading.ac.uk/web/FILES/special-collections/featuremicrographia.pdf.

9 Ibid.

10 Douglas Anderson, "Counting the Little Animals," Lens on Leeuwenhoek, accessed May 27, 2014, http://lensonleeuwenhoek.net/counting.htm.

41 Ari L. Goldman, "Eugene Odum, 88, Who Founded Modern Ecology, Dies," *New York Times*, August 14, 2002, http://www.nytimes.com/2002/08/14/obituaries/14ODUM.html.

GLOSSARY

erosion: the gradual wearing away of rock, soil, and other bits of earth. Erosion is caused by wind, water, and ice.

fossil: a trace or print or the remains of a long-ago organism preserved in earth or rock

heredity: the process of passing physical traits from parents to offspring

invertebrate: an animal without a backbone

molecule: the smallest particle of a substance that has all the characteristics of the substance

monastery: a building or group of buildings where a community of monks live

nucleus: a cell part in most organisms, necessary for heredity and for making proteins, that contains the chromosomes and is enclosed in a nuclear membrane

reproduction: the process by which organisms create offspring, or new organisms like themselves

sedimentation: the process of rock or dirt moving to a new place and forming a solid layer

species: a category of living things made up of related individuals that can mate and have offspring able to reproduce

technology: a machine, piece of equipment, or method designed by humans

theory: a principle or set of principles that explains how or why something happens

zoologist: a scientist who studies animals

SELECTED BIBLIOGRAPHY

Carter, J. Stein. "Ecology: History and Background." University of Cincinnati–Clermont College Biology Department. March 20, 2012. http://biology.clc.uc.edu/courses/bio303/history.htm.

Hollricher, Karin. "Quiet Pioneers." *Lab Times,* March 2013. Accessed May 28, 2014. http://www.labtimes.org/labtimes/issues/lt2013/lt03/lt_2013_03_16_21.pdf.

Levin, Simon A. "The Evolution of Ecology." *The Chronicle of Higher Education.* August 8, 2010. http://chronicle.com/article/The-Evolution-of-Ecology/123762/.

Mazzarello, Paolo. "A Unifying Concept: The History of Cell Theory." *Nature Cell Biology.* 1999. Accessed May 28, 2014. http://www.nature.com/index.html?file=/ncb/journal/v1/n1/full/ncb0599_E13.html.

Raven, Peter H., and George B. Johnson. "Chapter 13: Patterns of Inheritance." *Biology.* 6th ed. 2001. Accessed May 29, 2014. http://www.mhhe.com/biosci/genbio/raven6b/graphics/raven06b/other/raven06b_13.pdf.

Understanding Evolution for Teachers. University of California Museum of Paleontology. 2006. Accessed June 5, 2014. http://evolution.berkeley.edu/evosite/evohome.html.

FURTHER INFORMATION

Ballen, Karen Gunnison. *Decoding Our DNA: Craig Venter vs. the Human Genome Project.* Minneapolis: Twenty-First Century Books, 2013.
This book tells the explosive story of how ambition, greed, ego, and principle combined in the race to decode the human genome.

BrainPOP: Cells
http://www.brainpop.com/health/bodysystems/cells
At this interactive, animated website, visitors can learn all about cell structures and functions, watch movies about cells, play games, and take quizzes.

Evolution for Students
http://www.pbs.org/wgbh/evolution/students/index.html
Use this website's resources to think and talk about evolution more clearly.

Johnson, Sylvia A. *Shaking the Foundation: Charles Darwin and the Theory of Evolution.* Minneapolis: Twenty-First Century Books, 2013.
Follow the attempt to reconcile scientific fact with religious faith, from the earliest debates over Darwin's ideas to twenty-first-century controversies.

Kids Do Ecology
http://kids.nceas.ucsb.edu
Visit this website to learn more about ecology, data science, world biomes, and marine mammals.

Our Genes / Our Choices
http://www.pbs.org/inthebalance/archives/ourgenes/could_we.html
Explore the medical, legal, and ethical issues surrounding genetic research.

INDEX

PHOTO ACKNOWLEDGMENTS

The images in this book are used with the permission of: © Science Source, pp. 5, 8, 23 (both); © Print Collector/Hulton Archive/Getty Images, pp. 6 (top), 9; Courtesy of the National Library of Medicine, pp. 6 (left), 10, 21 (top), 16 (top right), 27 (right); © Universal History Archive/UIG/Bridgeman Images, pp. 6 (center), 11 (right), 36 (bottom), 39 (bottom); Henri Dutrochet, *Receherches Anatomiques et Physiologiques sur la Structure Intime des Animaux et des Végétaux, et sur Leur Motilité*, Paris: J-B Baillière, 1824, p. 6 (right); © Biophoto Associates/Photo Researchers/Getty Images, pp. 7 (left), 12; Bibliothèque Nationale de France/Wikimedia Commons, p. 7 (bottom); © SSPL via Getty Images, p. 7 (top); © Doug Struthers/Getty Images, pp. 7 (right), 14; © Stegerphoto/Photolibrary/Getty Images, p. 11 (left); © The Asahi Shimbun via Getty Images, p. 15; © DeAgostini/Getty Images, p. 16 (top); Wikimedia Commons, pp. 16 (bottom left), 20; © Power and Syred/ Science Source, pp. 16 (bottom right), 21 (bottom); © Spencer Sutton/Science Source, pp. 17 (left), 22; © iStockphoto.com/BeholdingEye, p. 17 (bottom); © Simon Fraser/Science Source, pp. 17 (bottom right), 24 (left); © James King-Holmes/Science Source, pp. 17 (right), 24 (right); Smithsonian Libraries/Biodiversity Heritage Library, p. 18; © iStockphoto.com/ Rawpixel, p. 19; Mary Evans Picture Library/Courtesy Everett Collection, p. 26 (top); © DEA/G. CIGOLINI/De Agostini/Getty Images, p. 26 (bottom left); Courtesy History of Science Collections, University of Oklahoma Libraries, pp. 26 (right), 27 (right), 30, 31, 36 (left center), 39 (top); © Private Collection/Bridgeman Images, pp. 27 (left), 30 (left); © Paul D Stewart/Science Source, pp. 27 (top), 32; © Werner Forman Archive/Bridgeman Images, p. 29; © Andreas Meyer/Shutterstock.com, p. 34; Zina Deretsky/National Science Foundation, p. 35; University of Illinois Archives, p. 36 (right); Charles Elton, *Animal Ecology*, The Macmillan Company, 1927, p. 37 (left); © Woodfall Wild Images/NHPA/ SuperStock, p. 37 (bottom); © John Loengard/The LIFE Picture Collection/Getty Images, pp. 37 (top), 42 (top); © Kip Evans/Alamy, p. 40; AP Photo/Scott Sonner, p. 42 (bottom).

Cover: © Volker Brinkmann/Visuals Unlimited, Inc.